CHILDREN'S CHOIR
BASICS

**Handbook for Planning, Developing and Maintaining
a Children's Choir in the Parish Community**

David T. Nastal

PASTORAL PRESS
PORTLAND · OREGON

ISBN 1-56929-032-6

© 1999 David T. Nastal
Pastoral Press
A Division of OCP Publications
5536 N.E. Hassalo
Portland, OR 97213
Phone: 800-LITURGY (548-8749)
Email: liturgy@ocp.org
Web site: www.pastoralpress.com
Web site: www.ocp.org

Library of Congress Cataloging-in-Publication Data

Nastal, David T., 1954-
     Children's choir basics: handbook for planning, developing, and main-
     taining a children's choir in the parish community / David T. Nastal.
          p. cm.
          ISBN 1-56929-032-6 (pbk.)
          1. Children's choirs. I. Title.

MT88 .N15 1999
782.7'7104 -- dc21   99-051359

Contents

Foreword   John Bertalot v

Chapter 1   Preparing the Ground 1

Chapter 2   Plan of Action 9

Chapter 3   Recruiting 15

Chapter 4   The Interview Process 23

Chapter 5   Preparing for Rehearsal 35

Chapter 6   The Rehearsal 43

Chapter 7   Tracking Progress 51

Chapter 8   The Choral Sound 57

Chapter 9   Repertoire 67

Chapter 10   Parents and Volunteers 77

Chapter 11   Expanding the Horizons 83

Chapter 12   Prayer Life of the Children's Choir 89

Appendix A   Basic Terms 96

Appendix B   Resources 100

Appendix C   Helpful Professional Organizations 104

Appendix D   Using a Metrical Index 106

Appendix E   Standard Hymns 109

Foreword

Foreword

I wish David Nastal could have written his superb book 40 years ago when I first began my career as a church musician, for I wouldn't have made so many thoughtless mistakes and I would have been able to achieve so much more so much sooner!

David and I met a few years ago when he attended a five-day choral workshop I was leading at Westminster Choir College in Princeton, New Jersey. During those fully packed sessions I shared everything I then knew about training singers of all ages and organizing choirs of all types and caring for their families — based, largely, on my two recently published books.

At one session dedicated to children's choirs, I asked the choral directors how many children there were in their choirs. A few had 10, some had 20 or 30, but one director had 150. "How did you attract 150 children into your choir program?" I asked. "By following the practical ideas in your books," he answered. "When I began my new job three years ago," he added, "I didn't have any children." This left us all speechless, so I hurried onto the choirmaster sitting next to him — it was David Nastal. "How many children do you have in your choir program?" I asked. "250," he answered with a smile. I don't remember what happened after that, for we were all so stunned by what he said. We were conscious of being in the presence of a church musician of exceptional pastoral and musical caliber.

Here is a book by a proven authority who has taken immense care to share deep insights and high standards with us all. What a gift to the whole church! If we implement his practical suggestions, it will be an ongoing blessing to all with whom we work.

This book is packed with so much practical information that you will need to read it again and again to make the many ideas come true for you in your choir program. From the hundreds of challenging thoughts that David shares, I've chosen four at random to whet your appetite:

1 *"If you don't like children, stop here."*

Yes! We cannot communicate with children unless we love them first or, at least, take initiative to like them. We may say the right words to our singers but nothing will get through to them unless they know that we respect them and expect great things of them. Children are especially quick to sense whether or not we really care for them.

If we don't have passion for what we teach and respect for the people we teach, we may as well be talking to a brick wall — and brick walls are notoriously unresponsive. The love of music, like Christianity, is caught rather than taught; we need to start with ourselves to make sure that we love the people committed to our care, and love the music we create with them. Thus, through the inspired words and marvelous music, they begin to experience a vision of God, love God with all their hearts and love their neighbors as themselves. For this reason, never sing anything but the best, for children respond wonderfully to the challenge of excellence.

2 *"Expand your vision."*

I know, from conducting my own choirs and watching colleagues all over the world conducting theirs, that the sky is the limit for children belonging to great choirs. They can do almost anything, given inspired, informed and loving leadership. They can learn to read music so quickly, sing high notes so easily, grow in confidence so rapidly, sing demanding solos so beautifully and bring along friends to join their choirs because they so fully enjoy the experience of singing. Many of these children, in turn, will bring along their families to become faithful church members. Church music is one of the church's most powerful tools for gospel proclamation. What is more, music can take us to the very gates of heaven itself.

When our young people graduate from high school — many of them will have stayed with us right though their teenage years — they and their families will bless us the rest of their lives for all they have gained through their choir work. One of my choir members in Princeton pointed out to me that choir directors influence young choristers even more than the presbyter or minister, because singers see them at close range so frequently. Let that influence be wholly for their good — it is an awesome responsibility.

3   *"Participants in children's choirs today will be the adults of the church tomorrow."*

This is true. The reason so many of us spend much of our lives making music in the church is that we were taken to join a church choir when we ourselves were young.

There's another side, too. Archbishop Carey said a few years ago when talking with young people in Washington National Cathedral, "Don't let anyone tell you that you are members of tomorrow's church, for you are not. You are members of today's church." How encouraged they must have been to hear those prophetic words!

During my 16 years as director of music at Trinity Episcopal Church, Princeton, I enjoyed the great privilege of creating glorious music with some of the most talented and intelligent musicians I have ever met, but the greatest privilege was to lead the choristers' weekly confirmation class. I thought that I was there to share God's love with them, but it was they who so often shared God's love with me. They were and are most lively members of today's church.

Yes, *yes,* YES! I have learned nearly all I know about choir training from watching others to see which ideas might work for me. From every one of them I learned something of immediate practical value — even, sometimes, what *not* to do — and I'm still learning. When one stops learning it's time to stop teaching.

But, because you have bought this book, you have shown that you want to continue to learn how to lead choirs even better, especially children's choirs. So start reading: Get out your highlighter to mark ideas that could work for you right now, and begin putting into practice the treasures that lie within these pages. They will illuminate your understanding and expand your vision of what is possible. Future generations of choristers and families will call you blessed!

Dr. John Bertalot

Assistant Regional Director, RSCM
Director of Music Emeritus, Trinity Church, Princeton NJ
Cathedral Organist Emeritus, Blackburn Cathedral, England
http://www.metanoia.org/johnbertalot

Preparing
the Ground

Preparing the Ground

"We plow the fields, and scatter the good seed on the land."

— M. Claudius, 1740–1815

Developing a children's choir program in a church community starts with a realistic look at available resources: your own enthusiasm and energy, the presence of enough children to make the idea viable, the support of parents, and the cooperation of the pastor, pastoral staff and other church leaders.

It begins with you. If you don't like children, stop here. A children's choir director must be genuinely interested in children and honestly enthusiastic about working with them. You will be spending a *lot* of time with them; they can spot a well-intentioned phony in a heartbeat. You will need patience, flexibility, physical energy, good musical skills, sturdy faith and a resilient spirit. You will teach, lead and communicate; in addition, at any given time, you will need the skills of a salesman, a public relations specialist or a politician. It comes with the territory.

If You're Not the Music Director

If you are not in charge of the overall parish music program, it is imperative that you have clear, direct communication with the music director. In the initial stages, it would be best to find a place where the two of you can talk for about an hour, uninterrupted by phone calls or other intrusions. A meeting away from the parish grounds can avoid "turf guarding." Share your ideas, dreams and philosophy; work out how a children's choir program will fit into the overall parish music ministry. Flexibility is needed, both for you and for the parish music director.

Develop mutual expectations and mutually beneficial exchanges of ideas. Never assume anything. You don't want to find out in December that the director is expecting a massive holiday production while your goal is simply to prepare the choir for a Christmas Eve liturgy. Be open to constructive criticism while pursuing excellence in musicianship and liturgy. Remember that you *must* have the support of the director, the pastor and other staff. Without that support, you may need to reevaluate your goals.

The Pastor

A crucial part of preparing the foundation is the initial meeting with the pastor, who is ultimately responsible for the parish. One pastor may be enthusiastic, another indifferent. This first meeting is to establish communication and to listen to the pastor's concerns. Share your philosophy about the importance of a children's choir program, of developing music ministry in the parish and of involving children in liturgy. Find out what the pastor's expectations are. If they differ from yours, how will you negotiate resolution? Listen carefully to what is being said — and what is not being said. Diplomacy and tact are extremely useful in "selling" a program; it's all part of the process. Keep the pastor fully informed at every stage of the development process.

Other key people to approach include the parish council, those responsible for religious education and those responsible for preparing liturgy; if the parish has a parochial school, talk to the principal and music teacher. Ask everyone for suggestions and advice. Listen attentively, take notes and gather information. Don't come on too strong; that can intimidate without your knowing it. Good communication with potential resource persons can build a cooperative spirit and develop allies.

Overview of the Community

It is wise to research the community's resources. A children's choir program might not be viable in a church that serves a retirement community or senior citizen center. A general overview of the demographics of the community can give you an idea of resources and limitations. Some questions to ask are:

> What is the median age of the community?
> What are the economic strata?
> Are parents willing to support arts and cultural experiences for their children?

A parish school can be a rich source of information. Early in the process, make an effort to communicate with the school music teacher; it's better to talk graciously than to trample on toes. It can take weeks, months, even years to heal damage done at this stage and regain trust.

Visit local elementary schools. If possible, arrange an interview with music teachers to discuss your plans for your program and to get advice and suggestions. One of your goals is to become known in the community as the children's choir director: it's free publicity for your program.

What are the general interests of the church and secular communities — sports, the arts, the military? The answers here can tell you how much groundwork will be necessary for a successful program. Obviously, the best of all possible worlds is a community with strong support of the arts; but educating the community to an understanding of artistic expression as a faith response is worthwhile and brings its own rewards.

Why a Children's Choir?

Now it's time to formulate a vision, a reason for having a children's choir program in this community at this time. The purpose of a children's choir is to develop children's musicianship, integrate them into parish music ministry and allow them authentic involvement in the community's prayer. This vision is always in the process of growth and change. Sort out the "whys" carefully so that you may present a clear vision. What are the pastoral needs for a children's choir? Using children only for special occasions such as Christmas and Easter is trite, and exploits their contribution. Expand the vision. Transform participation into a regular liturgical rhythm, contributing at scheduled parish liturgies such as Sunday Mass, Evening Prayer or monthly religious education events. Avoid commitments that "use" the children instead of supporting their contribution to the total community experience. Children's choirs are not for the entertainment of doting adults.

Look to the future. What changes will occur in your community over the next twenty years? Is the area growing? Shrinking? Participants in the children's choir will be the adults involved in ministry in the future church. What would you like the prayer and music to become? How do you envision the music ministry of the future? How do you plan to improve the standards of music, liturgy and education in the future ownership of the church? This is your opportunity to make a difference in the future. Do not treat it lightly.

What will directing a children's choir demand of you in terms of music education and development of artistic expression? Some children (and some communities) are more reluctant than others to participate in the arts. Your sensitive approach can change this. Don't sell children short because of their community's resistance; artistic expression can bloom even in limited and arid soil. Young ideas need encouragement, tender care, food and water. As director, you can be the catalyst for developing artistic expression in children — and in their parents; a children's choir program provides an excellent forum for dialogue.

Identify where you will find support in the parish. Where do you foresee major or minor conflicts? Being an ostrich doesn't work. Distinguish between areas you can change and problems that are insurmountable. Advance scheduling is important. Carefully look over the public school calendar and parish calendar. When are the Scout programs? What days of the week are most tightly scheduled for sports in the public schools? Don't wear yourself out; budget your commitments of energy and time, choosing your battles wisely.

As you can see, in order to build a sturdy program with vision, a children's choir director has to work in circles more extensive than just music. Like planting and nurturing delicate spring shoots that will blossom in summer's heat, the care taken in preparing the ground for the children's choir program will blossom in the future.

A Plan
of Action

Chapter 2

A Plan of Action

"We, your servants, bring the worship Not of voice alone,
but heart: Consecrating to your purpose.
Evr'y gift which you impart."

"Lord, Whose Love in Humble Service"
— Albert F. Bayly, 1901–1984

If developing a children's choir still seems like a realistic vision, it's time to sit down with pencil and paper, or computer, and write out a rationale. Why a children's choir? Why here? Why now? Include strategic areas of consideration: spiritual life, liturgical understanding, support and development of the religious education program and the future of the church.

Don't skip this step. These are legitimate questions that people will ask; you must be able to answer them clearly and purposefully if you want support for your program.

Musicians are well aware of the power of music to express the inner self. Working with the language of music can foster in children the beginnings of transcendent experiences; putting those experiences in a spiritual context can strengthen a child's belief in the constant presence of God. To a child just beginning his or her relationship with God, music is a valuable doorway into the richness of spiritual life.

A children's choir can give participants a deeper understanding of the community's liturgies; this understanding enhances the values children learn in the religious education program. A choir that sings not only for Mass but also for sacramental celebrations, such as baptism, first reconciliation and first communion, integrates children into the community's liturgical life.

It is no exaggeration to say that a children's choir can affect the future of both the local parish community and the broader church. The seeds of musicianship, discipline and spiritual life bear much fruit as children grow up, attend high school and college and, often, settle in another worship community. Children who have had positive musical experiences are more likely to become actively involved in music ministry and other ministries as adults. Many adults look back on their childhood choir experiences as a formative factor in deciding to participate in adult ministry. The opposite is also true; people whose musical experiences as children were unpleasant are often unenthusiastic about music ministry as adults. The ministry, musicianship and vision of the director are crucial.

Researching the Project

Resources are available from various publishing houses; see Appendix B for a listing. Much of the planning and curriculum work has been done in these manuals. All have scholarly contributors with extensive experience. You need to take a quiet week long before "kick-off" for a serious review of these programs. Many companies will send you a copy for a 14-day review period. Each program has its strengths and weaknesses. You will need to choose one that will fit your teaching style and the parish's worship needs, one that is theologically sound and reinforces the faith of the community. You may need to borrow from more than one series to arrive at a training program that will work in your particular situation, in the same way that a tailor-made suit sometimes fits better, wears longer and receives more compliments. When selecting a program, remember that this is a long-range project; allow three to five years for results to show within the choir.

Part of the education of a children's choir director consists of interviewing other directors who have successful programs. Most directors are eager to share advice and recount their own successes and failures. How do they approach teaching a new song or a new musical concept? Be an active listener and listen carefully; in the months and years ahead, they could become close and valued colleagues. Those who build professional camaraderie, nurturing and supporting one another, are more likely to survive the inevitable difficulties with grace and patience. The best advice often passes from director to director over a cup of coffee. As your program develops, you may want to set up a regular forum, such as an informal potluck meal, for local children's choir directors to exchange ideas and share problems.

Observing other directors in action is a must. Take notes: what skills are successful before, during and after rehearsal? Note their musicianship, their alertness in observing the children, their directing style. You will need to develop these skills yourself. How do they interact with children? What works? What makes children uncomfortable, or diminishes their enthusiasm? What techniques produce desirable tones and good breath support? Children will give one hundred percent when they are led correctly and confidently, encouraged lovingly and held to a clear standard. Is that what you are observing in rehearsal? Not all advice is good; you will have to distill what you hear and see into a style that is effective for you.

In addition to observing other directors, you have homework to do with parents, teachers and other professionals. Gather parents in small groups, perhaps after liturgy or during religious education times. Share your ideas and excitement and enlist their input, vision and support. You cannot do this without them! If parents take ownership of the program, half your battles are already won.

Articulating Your Vision

Putting your vision into words is important. Take the time to pray about this, asking yourself questions. How will a children's choir program affect the spiritual life of the community? How can I help these children participate more actively at Sunday liturgy? What effect will this program have on the children's understanding of Jesus' love and presence in their lives? Reflect quietly with pencil in hand.

Outline what you would like to see happen with the program in a year. In three years. In five years. The wagon trains heading out to settle the American West had a vision, a sense of direction: They were heading west, knew what they were leaving behind and to what they were looking forward. You need to have your own wagon train heading toward your vision. When your goals are clearly defined, in your mind and on paper, they will help greatly with the start-up work as well as with the evaluation process at the end of the year.

Two more questions: Are your goals for the first year realistic? Can your goals be accomplished *in this community?* You won't be finished with this part of the process until the answer to both these questions is "Yes!" The answers depend on how well you know your community, how receptive the church is and how well the ground has been prepared.

Recruiting

Chapter 3

Recruiting

"Come with me into the fields."

— Dan Schutte, b. 1947

Now the hard work starts: recruiting. Searching for choristers is not an easy task in a society that places heavy demands on children's time. It also can be an uphill battle to create interest in a new program with no track record.

The first step is to survey the children in the parish. You are the program's public relations director! Get out there and be seen — by children, parents and community leaders. Talk with children, not just about music; learn their names and get to know what interests them. When you let them become acquainted with you, some of the mystery of the program dissolves. Write personal notes acknowledging non-music achievements.

No children's choir director ever added water, stirred and came up with a perfect choir of fifty children who read music and had good intonation. Every director has to motivate children (to join), parents (to support) and pastors (to appreciate publicly).

Some children will be eager to join because of positive music experiences elsewhere, in church or in school. Some will join because their friends are joining; others will join because of parental involvement. Involving, motivating and engaging today's children takes creative thought: invite a well-established children's choir to perform a concert at your parish, or organize a field trip for interested parents and children to a children's choir concert in another church or at a nearby

Sample Cover Letter

St. Catherine
1234 SE Street
Anywhere, USA 0000

Dear Parent or Guardian,

My name is Joseph Marvin. I would like to share with you the idea of a new music ministry program beginning at St. Catherine and ask for your involvement.

St. Catherine is planning to begin a children's choir program that would include children in grades 2–5. According to the parish records, Louise is eligible to become involved in this program. Enclosed is a brochure that explains the program and outlines the time commitments. I ask you to review this brochure and talk with Louise about this program.

During the week of Aug. 23 through Aug. 30, parent volunteers will be calling you to help answer any questions you may have as well as to set up an interview with you and your child. If you have immediate questions, please feel free to contact me at 555-3939. I look forward to hearing from you!

Sincerely,

Joseph Marvin
Music Director (*or* Children's Choir Director)

symphony hall. Selling the program is important, but be careful: children will pick up on anything trite or patronizing — and that's the first step down the road to disaster.

Programs that gather children are already in place in the parish. The religious education program should be one of your first visits. Here you can sense the children's general feelings and interest regarding church. Schedule time in the classroom to talk with the children about the children's choir program; make your pitch to the parents waiting to pick up their children after class. Make these visits brief, but memorable; don't go on and on. Spark their interest, hand out a registration form and give them an attractive informational brochure about the program. If the parish has a school, ask if you can address the classes. Again, pique their interest; leave them eager to learn more about the program. Don't forget summer parish education programs and special projects where children are present.

Children are present at Sunday liturgies, at ball games, shopping and parish picnics. Talk with them and their parents after Mass or during coffee and doughnuts.

Reach Out and Touch Someone

Since nearly all parishes are computerized these days, ask permission to search the parish database. If you're not computer literate, enlist the support of the parish administrative assistant whose ongoing cooperation you need. A data search for a selected age bracket can give you a wealth of names to draw from. If the budget permits, mail the informational brochure to the parents with a cover letter about the focus of the children's choir program and what will be expected of the choristers. Mention that there will be a follow-up phone call within the week to talk about the program and answer questions they may have.

Personal follow-up phone calls — from the director or a group of supportive parents — are extremely productive; they provide an opportunity for personal contact and conversation with parents, as well as for good public relations about music ministry in general. You may find a parent who might be interested in joining the adult choir. This part of the process is very time-consuming, but the benefits are well worth the effort.

A word of caution: this is telemarketing. Use it wisely. Outline a dialogue for volunteer callers to use, along with program facts and information. Callers should know the name of the person being called and immediately identify themselves, their affiliation with the church and the reason for the phone call. A good opening reference is the informational letter sent out earlier. Keep index cards handy, so that you and your volunteer callers can note who responds eagerly or who might be interested in other areas of ministry. Each interested response should be followed up by an interview with the director.

Church bulletins, newsletters, bulletin boards, posters and pulpit announcements are traditional ways of publicizing a program. These informational announcements are helpful in getting the word out — but the most effective recruiting tool is personal contact.

Parent-to-parent communication is another part of the recruiting process. Parents are strongly invested in their children's activities; they talk with one another around the sports field or swimming pool. Get them talking to one another about the children's choir program. You may want to host an adult information gathering some evening or on a Sunday after liturgy.

Plan a Music Ministry Sunday for the parish; involve adult choir members and musicians in recruiting for the children's choir. Name tags or buttons that say, "I am a music minister — ask me a question!" can break the ice.

The Brochure

One of the strongest tools for solid advertising and promoting the children's choir program is the informational brochure. This is the program's calling card: it should include a *brief* summary of the philosophy and purpose of the children's choir program, general information, rehearsal schedule and performance/liturgy commitments, a brief biographical note about the director and special events for the choir. Keep it clear and short; too much information can be confusing, even overwhelming. Produce the most attractive, eye-catching, professional brochure that you possibly can. A flimsy, error-ridden brochure gives a negative message. Make sure someone with an eagle eye proofreads it before it goes to be printed.

In addition to mailing brochures to church members with eligible children, brochures should be available in the church commons or vestibule and pamphlet racks. Pass them out to students in the school and religious education program. The YMCA, the Catholic Youth Organization, Boys and Girls Clubs and sports programs are other venues where brochures can be made available.

If your parish has a web site, use it to promote the program. Community members who work in public relations might be willing to assist with the recruiting process for the choir as well as with church ministry in general.

Sample Brochure

PERFORMANCE SCHEDULE

[How often will the choir sing? At what liturgy?]

The Children's Choir sings on the [second Sunday] of the month during the school year at the [11 A.M.] liturgy.

Specific times and dates are posted at the beginning of each term, as well as being announced in the church bulletin.

PARENTAL INVOLVEMENT

Parents are a vital part of the Children's Choir program. You are always welcome to observe rehearsal, but parents with small children are asked to remain in the common area during rehearsal. At various times during the year, helping hands are needed for projects and progra[...] and wish t[...] contact th[...]

SPECIAL EVENTS

Although singing for liturgy is primary, as the Children's Choir program grows and as choristers become more experienced, concerts, services of lessons and carols, and other events may be added.

As the Children's Choir members progress in musicianship and liturgical knowledge, they are assigned roles of responsibility. Some choristers will help younger children prepare, while others may eventually serve as cantors at liturgy or as assistants to the director.

ABOUT THE DIRECTOR

The Children's Choir program is under the direction of [name, brief bio of educational background and experience.]

CHILDREN'S CHOIR PROGRAM

[name of church]
[address]

CHILDREN'S CHOIR REGISTRATION FORM

Child's Name _____

Address _____ Zip _____

Parent(s) Name _____ Phone _____

School _____ Grade _____ Birthday _____

Registration Fee: $ _____ per child for music and materials
Please make checks payable to [name of your church].

ABOUT CHILDREN'S CHOIR

The goal of the Children's Choir program is to teach children the language of music and artistic expression within the context of a Catholic Christian community of faith, which includes active and regular participation in church liturgies.

Participants in the Children's Choir program are actively involved in the spiritual and liturgical life of the church. They serve as ministers of music at selected liturgies throughout the year.

ABOUT THE CURRICULUM

[Proofread everything very carefully!]

The Children's Choir program is committed to fostering excellent musicianship, knowledgeable participation in liturgy and an active prayer life. These will include ongoing music theory, ear training and sight singing; fundamentals of liturgy and involvement in the prayer life of the community.

THE OBJECTIVES OF CHILDREN'S CHOIR

[You can use this, or insert your own.]

The objective of the Children's Choir program at [name of your church] is best summed up by Ruth Krehbiel Jacobs, founder of the National Choristers Guild:

Training the worship attitude of our children is like tending a rare plant. The seed must first be planted and the soil kept in a condition that encourages growth. Once the seed has been planted, it requires patient care until it reaches full flower. When it does put forth a bud, fragrant with the richness of true worship, we may be humbly grateful for the privilege of having been the gardeners.

THE SCHEDULE

[Determine your schedule well in advance, so that it can go into the brochure.]

The Children's Choir rehearses in the worship center on Tuesdays from 6:00 to 7:00 p.m.

Weekly rehearsals begin the Tuesday after Labor Day and continue until Christmas break. Regular rehearsals resume after New Year's Day and conclude with the spring concert.

A detailed schedule will be available in September; it will include dates and times of the choir's expected attendance at liturgies and concerts.

The
Interview
Process

The Interview Process | Chapter 4

"Here I am, Lord. Is it I, Lord?"

— Dan Schutte, b. 1947

A children's choir program involves choristers, parents and director in a triangle. In order to grow, the program needs the support of all three or it will run out of steam. The previous chapters will have given you an idea whether you, the prospective director, are up to this task. Now you need to engage the interest, support and active involvement of both child and parent.

It's often easier to "sell" the program to an energetic, interested child than to a stressed-out, over-committed parent. Involve the parent *gently*. Be warned: Without parental support, attendance at rehearsals and performances will be sporadic.

During the recruiting phase, you've gathered names and taken the time to get to know each child and parent in person and by phone. You've given them the outline of the responsibilities and commitment required of a chorister in the program. You've developed a printed brochure of expectations and important calendar dates.

As recruiting continues, start scheduling interviews with prospective choristers and their parent(s). ("Interview" is a less intimidating word than "audition.") Interviews should be scheduled at least two, and not more than three, weeks before the first rehearsal. Applicants should be notified within 48 hours of their interview whether they are accepted, accepted on probation or not accepted. Mid-season interviews also can be held after Christmas, a week before rehearsals resume; in this case, choristers should be notified of their status within 24 hours.

Even the most promising walk-in should be interviewed before being invited to join. Yes, it's time-consuming, but don't skimp. You may want to set up interviews with two or three children in the same time frame in order to reduce their anxiety; this can be a great ice-breaker for both children and parents. Allow no longer than twenty minutes for each interview: three minutes with the parent; ten minutes with the child; from five to seven minutes with parent and child together.

At the interview, welcome child and parent with honest warmth, exuding confidence and energy. You want this meeting to provide the answers to three questions: How well does the child identify pitch? What is the range of the voice? Is there evidence of support for the singing voice?

Keep the interview upbeat. A grim, "this-is-a-test" approach will finish off your program before it starts. Do your own homework: know something about area sports programs, school music departments or local children's theatre. Get the chorister talking about his or her interests. Ask questions; show your own keen interest. Who are the child's favorite music performers? Is the child involved in a science or math competition? Are there brothers and sisters? Are they involved in music? Is the prospective chorister already taking part in a music program or production at school or in the community? This preliminary discussion allows you to evaluate the child's enthusiasm for the arts, especially music, and gives you insight into personal interests and musical abilities.

At this point, is the child excited about music? Or do you sense too heavy a dose of parental pressure? It's a tough judgment call. Music comes from the heart: it needs to be evoked and coaxed out, not squeezed and pulled. Tensions and pressures not addressed here will surface later. Be sensitive to the child's anxiety level. This is a major step; it may possibly be the first time the child has moved forward as an individual.

Your calm confidence and relaxed manner will encourage each child to do his or her best.

Keep the child talking about *anything*, especially music, while you observe, observe, observe. Is the child's body language shy? Confident? How much "free time" does the child have? Does he spend most of his time in front of the computer? Is she a team player? Music making is a group effort requiring team skills. Listen to the range and resonance of the child's speaking voice. How are the vocal cadences and phrasing? Are answers monosyllabic, or is the child making an effort to converse? Music making requires mind, body and spirit — another triangle to keep in mind!

You can formulate your own questions for music evaluation. It would be wise to find out if prospective choristers take private music lessons or are involved in a school music program; if so, will those rehearsals or recitals limit their participation in the children's choir program at church?

Rhythm

The next step in the interview is using echo clapping to assess the child's rhythmic talent. Start with simple rhythmic patterns using quarter and eighth notes, progressing through more complex patterns that use simple syncopation. Do not underestimate children's abilities; it is amazing how rap music has increased their vocabulary of complex rhythms. However, walk them through slowly, step by step, progressing logically to the more difficult patterns.

Play or sing a short melody and have the child clap the rhythm of the melody back to you. You might include rhythm chants with catchy patterns from hymns or songs. Involve the child in the creative process: let them give you a few patterns. Be alert — the patterns they give you may be more complex than you are prepared for!

Singing

At last! Choose a song familiar to the child, such as "Happy Birthday," "My Country, 'Tis of Thee" or a song or hymn known from church. (This is *not* the time to teach a new melody.) Singing together with the child will help break the ice; then you can ask the child to sing alone. Consider volleying phrases of the song back and forth, with you singing one phrase, the child singing the next, and so on. What type of tone is being produced? Is the child's breath supporting the tone? Is the tone on pitch — or close to it?

At this point, you are only looking at the basic vocal material. The children don't have to be perfect. You will be able to deal with most minor problems and give them the experience of successful choral singing. Don't expect a finished product at this stage. What you are listening for is how well the child finds the pitch; it's less important if the child finds the pitch in the wrong octave or has a weak sound.

Exercises

Here are some specific exercises from which to choose — they need not take more than three or four minutes — when looking for particular musical skills:

— Sing a "ho-ha" (1-5-1, do-sol-do) pattern up the scale by half-steps to determine range.

— Get the child to laugh like Santa to determine breath support. A bit of joking can make this exercise fun while allowing you to find out the range of the child's voice.

— Let the child give you a pitch to sing. After a few of these, reverse roles: you "throw" the pitch to the chorister and ask the child to return it. If it is not on pitch, try another one. Use baseball terms such as "Out" or "Foul ball," especially if the child is involved with Little League.

— Have the child blow up a balloon. It can't be done without using the diaphragm muscle to exhale, so the balloon provides a quick and easy way to see if the child uses or knows how to use the diaphragm.

— Have the child take a breath through a drinking straw to experience using the diaphragm to inhale.

— Have the child take a "drinking straw" breath and ask them to make a candle flame dance without blowing out the candle. This is tricky, but children love it!

Video games have limited children's attention span and ability to concentrate. The creative director can meet this challenge by making things fun. Have the child "hum like the bees" as you check for focus and resonance, and "hoot like the owls" to assess range and an open tone. Often a child will be afraid to use the head voice because so much music on radio uses chest voice sounds; hooting like an owl or using fire engine sounds can help a child break into head voice. Yawning and arm-stretching help relax the throat and produce an open tone.

During these exercises, stay alert. What is the feeling in the room? Is the child edgy or overly serious? (More laughter may be needed.) Is the child enjoying the interaction and making music? Producing relaxed tones? Focus on the child, but keep an eye on the parent's reaction and input. Give the child every opportunity to make successful choices, even if the alternate choices are ridiculous. Children hear "No!" all too frequently, at school and at home. Give questions in an "a-or-b" format: Is it wise or unwise? Do we fill the room with sound or project our voice?" (You will use this same strategy in rehearsals.) As children come to understand the concepts, you can ask more intricate questions; but always keep the child involved in choosing and evaluating. An active mind engaged in making music forestalls mountains of discipline problems.

Parents

Parents are an integral part of the interview process. What are their talents and interests? What is their musical background? Can you engage their talents and gifts in support of the music program? One parent may be able to take charge of a specific project; another may be an accompanist willing to assist at rehearsals and performances. Another may be able to help children with limited skills. Telephone trees, music filing — the creative director will look for every possible way to interest and involve parents. (See Chapter 9.)

Talk to parents and children together about the time commitment. Be as specific as possible about rehearsals and liturgies, but avoid an overwhelming list of dates and performances — at least for the first year. Listen carefully to the concerns of both parent and child. In this portion of the interview, you may discover a drastic conflict between the rehearsal schedule and the ball team or school schedule. You may need to find a more accessible rehearsal time.

Making the Cut

One of the most difficult things a choir director must do is decide who makes the cut. Coaches, teachers and school principals all face the same dilemma. The basic question is "Who has the gifts and the talents to be a part of this group?" The easy decisions are those who are naturally gifted. The difficult decisions fall into three categories:

- The child is interested, but needs help with pitch or rhythm.
- The child is deeply interested, but lacks music skills and has a short attention span.
- The child is not interested, or lacks aptitude, but is being pushed by a "musical" parent.

Someone needs to reach out to these children — but, as director, you have to balance the needs of the whole group in the time available for rehearsals, teaching and preparation. You may simply not have the time and energy. You cannot be all things to all people and expect to stay sane enough to deal with a choir program. Perhaps a talented parent could work with the children of limited skills, preparing them to join the main group after nine to twelve weeks of very basic skill training. Setting up such a pre-placement or probationary group allows the inclusion of more children.

Before you say "No" to a child, make sure you have tried every angle possible and considered the needs of your particular community. Cultivate tact. Anger or disappointment can become public and negative. Negative talk in a community can prove a major setback for the choir program, especially in the first year.

Preparing
for
Rehearsal

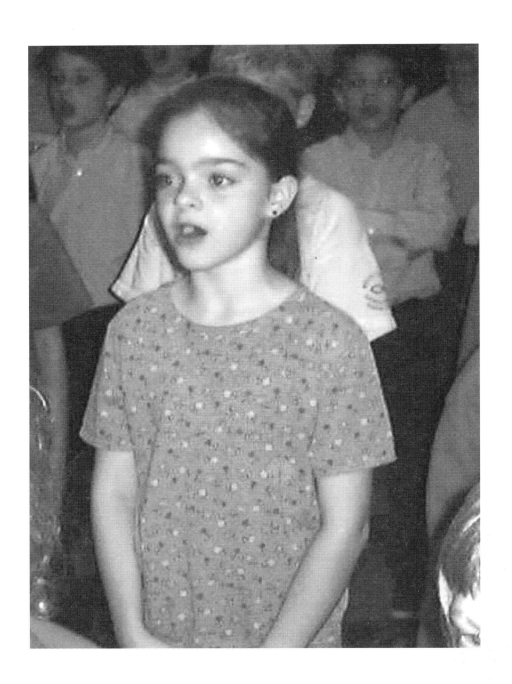

Preparing for Rehearsal | Chapter 5

"Sing, choirs of angels, sing in exultation."

"O Come, All Ye Faithful"
— John Francis Wade, 1711–1786

The repertoire

The bedrock of a choir program is solid, suitable repertoire.
Deciding on the first year's repertoire is not an easy task.
Talk to other directors who have well-established, respected
programs in your area; they have already tilled and
weeded their first year's garden and can give you
numerous helpful tips.

You will need to tailor the choir program to the musical
abilities of the interviewed choristers, the prayer life of the
community and the demands of the liturgical calendar.
Keeping a balance will become easier with time, but in the
meantime you need to survive the first year. Be open to a
diversity of experiences, such as styles of music and ways of
teaching, listening and learning, both for yourself and for the
choristers. Handled openly, honestly and prayerfully, these
experiences will provide formation and growth.

There are numerous sources of children's music, but finding
music that has the "right fit" for your choir is a tough job,
particularly for a new group with no previous musical
identity or style. Do not limit the repertoire to "children's
music." Hymns, service music and responsorial psalms
should be an integral part of any children's choir repertoire.
Many hymns can be augmented with descants or secondary
harmony lines; some can be sung in rounds. The verses of a
responsorial psalm can provide a challenge for strong singers,

with the choir responding in two- or three-part harmony on the antiphon. The psalms should be part of every choir's sung prayer and reflection.

Getting Organized

Director's plan of action A rehearsal will flounder without a plan of action tempered with flexibility. Children perform well, and many discipline problems are forestalled, with a regular pattern of procedure; keep the pattern constant, changing it only if a real need becomes evident. Always start on time, even if only one child is present; and always end on time.

Folder Make sure each child has a personal folder marked with his/her name (or identity number for music filing purposes).

Attendance chart Procedures that the children can do on their own give them ownership of the process. Depending on age, they might be able to check themselves in on an attendance chart. A quick glance at the chart allows the director to track those who attend regularly and those who may need a follow-up phone call for unexcused absences. A parent might be able to help with these follow-up calls and keep the director apprised of why the chorister is missing rehearsal.

Bulletin board It's very useful to have a bulletin board or chalk board that the children check on a regular basis; this trains the children to be "bulletin board readers" and avoids numerous announcements during precious rehearsal time. (This also reinforces their alertness at school to special event notices on bulletin boards, which often go unnoticed.)

Discipline

Working with children requires that your personal style of discipline be true and honest. Any false action or lack of follow-through will be noted carefully by both child and parent. The cardinal rule is: be consistent! A regular rehearsal routine establishes the parameters of acceptable behavior and provides the children with a sense of security. Make the boundaries clear, and address unacceptable behavior immediately. Be gentle, firm and positive in giving correction. A child's life is filled with "No!"s. Avoid using that word during rehearsal; constantly look for the positive or, at least, use words that give correction without the cutting "no."

It cannot be stressed enough that a consistent pattern is a key element. Fluctuations lead to disaster in future rehearsals. In difficult situations, always avoid pre-judgment based on past experiences. Approach every child, every time, with a clean slate. Listen openly, ask questions and review with the child and parent what behavior is acceptable in choir. Even a discipline problem can be a learning experience for all concerned; it depends on how the initial steps are handled. For example: Susie pushes Johnny. Move them to opposite ends of the room; keep them after rehearsal; ask questions and help them resolve the issue. If conflict continues, call the parents and ask them to talk to the children; something else may be going on. Don't blow it!

One of the simplest ways to ensure good discipline is to space the children properly: not less than an arm's length from each other, side to side *and* front to back. They should not be able to touch one another. No poking, no prodding means no rehearsal disruption. You may have to make arrangements to hold rehearsals in the church rather than in a small classroom where space is limited, but the results will be worth the effort. Choristers who are physically apart learn to sing independently, not just follow along. When they sit closer together for liturgy or a performance, their sound automatically becomes fuller and livelier.

Singers who stand produce a much better tone than wiggly youngsters slumping in their seats. There are pros and cons to having chairs in the rehearsal space. Well-spaced chairs can define the child's physical limits and prevent discipline problems. Floor space can provide a relaxed atmosphere for choirs who sing standing but are allowed to sit on the floor during the five-question breaks. You may be able to use the design of the floor, or masking tape or carpet squares, to define the space. The more clearly defined the space, the more comfortable the child will be — and you won't have to keep repeating instructions on posture and discipline. It's a choice for the director: What type of rehearsal room atmosphere works best for both this group and the director's personal style?

Remember, a child who is interested and actively involved in the music making process is not a discipline problem. Your demanding and difficult job is to keep the children interested and motivated. All music making requires discipline to maintain high standards and a sense of success. Fair, consistent rehearsal discipline will develop loving respect between choristers and director. Asking questions, giving the children choices and keeping their minds engaged will lead to a smoothly running rehearsal.

Attendance

A child may wish to be part of the group, or want to experience the thrill of making music — but they have to *be* there for this to happen. If the group is going to grow musically, spiritually and socially, attendance at rehearsals is imperative. Do not be afraid to make your attendance expectations clear to both parents and children from the very beginning. Coaches demand it of their athletes; scout leaders require it of scouts. Choristers are no different.

Today's children live in a busy world, with all kinds of experiences. Conflicts with other activities should be discussed during the interview process, so that these do not present problems during the rehearsal season. Ask the parent how other activities will be balanced in relation to the choir commitment. Will the choir activity fit comfortably in the child's weekly schedule or will it be the last straw, the one that breaks the parent's back? Make clear what you will accept as an excused absence and also what constitutes an unexcused absence. Have the child contact you regarding absences; parents are helpful in implementing this. Unexcused absences should be noted and followed up with a phone call immediately. This demonstrates your concern, and reinforces the chorister's responsibility to the group. Each child is a player vital to the team, no matter what his or her musical role in the choir; the group is lessened by their absence. No matter how large or small the choir, each person in it is necessary, and every absence is a loss to the group.

The
Rehearsal

Chapter 6 | The Rehearsal

"Let us walk with each other in perfect harmony."

— Sy Miller, 1908–1941,
and Jill Jackson, 1955

SAMPLE REHEARSAL SCHEDULE

4:45 p.m. Choristers arrive, collect music, follow check-in procedures, use the restroom.

5:00 p.m. Rehearsal begins *promptly*, no matter how many singers are present. Use warm-ups with new anthem in mind. Include singing of familiar song or hymn.

5:09 p.m. Five-question break (one minute, *max*)

5:10 p.m. Sing familiar hymn, song or service music. Listen carefully and fix what needs fixing: diction, intonation and texts of specific verses.

5:15 p.m. Work on new anthem in small sections. Reinforce warm-ups.

5:25 p.m. Sing a familiar hymn tune or song, especially the second or third verse.

5:29 p.m. Five-question break

5:30 p.m. Work on second new anthem; introduce completely and work on small sections.

5:40 p.m. Polish a third anthem for the next liturgical responsibility (Sunday liturgy or other event).

5:54 p.m. Five-question break

5:55 p.m. Announcements; public testing of choristers for achievement levels; closing prayer and dismissal procedures.

6:00 p.m. Brief meeting with parents or choristers with extended questions. Close-up details with head choristers.

Warm-ups

Any good athlete knows that a warm-up reduces risk of injury and prepares the muscles for the task at hand. Children in a choir rehearsal need the same care and preparation. Sing warm-ups without excuses or exceptions. Keep the process engaging and entertaining for the children. If you are lucky enough to have one, a gifted chorister with strong music skills can demonstrate the warm-up exercises. Children will imitate a good sound, and a child's voice is easier for them to imitate than an adult voice. This kind of teaching can spark great interest and excitement, as well as gentle competition, among the children. It can also assist in developing head voice singing technique.

Staples

Every rehearsal should include the singing of hymns, songs, psalms and responses used at liturgy. These are the staples of the worshiping community and should become part of the regular music vocabulary for the children's choir. (During the first rehearsal, listen to and evaluate the sound of the group during this common ground.) Avoid overkill: the children are not just assembly additions, but need other music to develop their identity as children's choir.

Teaching an Anthem

In your own preparation, you should have watched other conductors analyze and teach an anthem. Well before rehearsal, analyze the anthem you will be teaching during this rehearsal. Know where the repeated sections are and which phrases will be difficult. Draw warm-up exercises from the anthem, using sequential phrases as vocalises, e.g., *"Gloria"* from "Angels We Have Heard on High," ascending by half steps. When introducing a song to the choir, present it in its entirety, either by playing and singing it, or by playing a recording; it's easier to get where you're going if you know where you are headed.

A quality recording, which demonstrates the desired musicianship, is a good first step. Be selective about the use of recordings, however; some children's choirs produce tones that will not support your vision for the choir. Keep your standards high and avoid sloppy singing. Exposing choristers to the quality singing of the best choirs develops their "listening ears"; and their own quality will improve.

After the overview, break the anthem into teachable sections and phrases. From the beginning, teach the children how to read the musical language. Take small steps, be consistent, and help them learn to "read" the music. Are there repeated sections? Where are the difficult passages? Teaching by rote is the easy way out; it's like going to a fast food restaurant — quick, but not healthy in the long run. Teaching sight reading and musicianship is a longer route, but you will reap the rewards in later rehearsals. There are several different methodologies for teaching sight singing; some of these resources are noted in the appendix.

Rehearsal Tempo

Most children, second grade and up, can handle a 40- to 60-minute rehearsal with ease if you come prepared. Always keep rehearsal moving; this can be a do-or-die situation! Always have something up your sleeve to move forward if things get stuck, but keep the overall pattern consistent, so that the children know what to expect. Video games and technology have decreased children's attention span but improved their reaction time. It might be wise to pace your rehearsal in ten-minute segments with "five-question breaks." (See Sample Rehearsal Schedule, above and Five-Question Breaks, below.) Over time you are trying to increase the children's concentration and improve their focus on music making. Rap music and MTV make this an uphill battle, but use their methods — brevity, liveliness, diversity, visual and aural presentation — in your rehearsal. Make it an experience to which the children can relate.

Vary styles at all rehearsals to prevent boredom and increase the music vocabulary. Mix Mozart with Dufford, Gregorian chant with African folk songs, Latin with Spanish, Handel with Copland! Balance is the key to successfully focused diversity.

As well as varying styles, vary the accompaniments for the children's voices. Use a piano or organ for giving pitches or accompaniment, but do not be afraid to sing a cappella (unaccompanied). Singing without accompaniment allows children to hear their own voices and those of the other children. Rounds and canons are very effective; you may already have one or more possibilities in your repertoire. Look at the index of your hymnal or songbook (or accompaniment manual) for tunes that can be sung in canon. Singing a round is an enjoyable way for the choir to begin singing parts.

Woodwind instruments work extremely well with children's voices. Flutes can help with intonation problems more quickly and more easily than an electronic keyboard. Flute descants can also be used in working with two-part harmony training. Add a guitar for harmonic rhythms and you have a Renaissance ensemble in contemporary style.

If your community is fortunate enough to have handbells, use them with your children's choir. Don't be shy. The bells help provide rhythmic clarity and harmonic confidence. If Orff instruments are available (through the church school or nearby public school), use them; these instruments can add excitement to the program while developing the children's musicianship. Summer programs in Orff instruments can benefit your choir program once you have gotten it off the ground. Rhythm instruments can also contribute to musicianship, but insist on a musical standard of playing the instruments, not just banging out rhythms. You are training musicians, not construction workers.

Don't limit your options. A child who studies a musical instrument may be able to play with the choir or even write out his or her own descant on melody. Keep children involved as active contributors and you will be amazed where this leads you — and your choir.

Five-Question Break

The five-question break is one way to organize a rehearsal. Children are always full of questions about anything and everything. Let them have the floor for five questions, preferably about music or what you've been working on — but in the long run, anything should be fair game. Holding their questions for these one-minute breaks helps children remain focused during rehearsal. It's advisable to plan five or six of these breaks per rehearsal.

Here are some examples of questions for the break: What are we wearing for the concert? What does this funny sign in the music mean? Why are you wearing the Bugs Bunny tie? Why is Sara wearing a special medal? What hymn book are we using Sunday?

Close the five-question break with one question from the director to reinforce a musical idea of the anthem being rehearsed: "On page 10, there's a funny sign with an F in it. Does that mean fast? Or forte?" Remember to keep to the question-answer format; this engages the child's thinking process. As the group matures in musicianship and concentration, these break periods may be diminished and replaced by information on bulletin boards and handout sheets. Avoid endless spoken announcements; children simply won't remember them all. Being creative in the way you dispense vital information will limit the number of questions from both choristers and parents. Questions not answered in the five-question break can be dealt with at the end of rehearsal. As rehearsal ends, give the children a good feeling of musical accomplishment: another familiar song or anthem, or repetition of a section you worked on earlier. Dismiss the group the same way for every rehearsal. A brief prayer particularly suited for children is in order. You might have the group construct a prayer or use intercessory prayer. Develop specific, orderly routines for ending rehearsal and use them every time.

Tracking Progress

Chapter

Tracking Progress

"Our footsteps God shall safely guide
To walk the ways of peace."

"Canticle of Zachary"
— tr. James Quinn, S.J., b. 1919

In addition to the vision and goals discussed earlier, the children's choir director needs a way to assess children's achievement. Members of children's liturgical choirs advance in three dimensions: music skills, liturgical understanding and spiritual development.

Musicianship is of prime importance in music ministry. The director needs to be aware of each child's level of musicianship. Holding the chorister accountable is like a coach's evaluation of an athlete's performance after games, practices or competitions. (Observe a Little League or soccer practice; you might be surprised at how strictly the children are held accountable for their performance.) The choir should be no different. Setting a high standard for choristers and tracking their progress can be a daunting task. Your ongoing interest in each child's growth results in respect and trust from the child, and improvement of the choir's overall musicianship.

Musical Skills

Does the child know how to support the tone, or is it airy and under pitch? Do choristers know the value of quarter, half and whole notes? Can they demonstrate this knowledge? You, their director, are responsible for imparting musical knowledge in an engaging way that will stick in their minds. In preparing for rehearsal, use the repertoire to illustrate and reinforce music theory, building their knowledge step by step. Avoid a staid classroom atmosphere when dealing with music theory; children are already experiencing that atmosphere for six hours or more a day. Use creative approaches to concepts: games, questions-and-answer sessions, contests and pre-rehearsal musical skill games. Maintain a high level of energy, interest and motivation. Without it, rehearsals stagnate and choristers drift away.

Liturgical Understanding

The child's understanding of liturgy is of equal importance to musicianship. The children's choir is part of the music ministry of the parish, which is part of the diocesan church, which is part of the universal church. Take the time to share your knowledge and your love for the liturgy. Read the Vatican II liturgy documents and some scholarly books on the liturgy, as well as children's textbooks that share liturgical perspectives. Talk with the director(s) of religious education and church pastor(s); perhaps they could schedule a ten-minute visit to your rehearsal. A visit from the pastor imparts a sense of worth to music ministry members, no matter what their age. Asking questions and exchanging ideas are a valuable experience for the children.

Visits by the church pastor(s) during liturgical seasons can help underscore the change of seasons and increase knowledge of what the season is about: preparation times (Advent and Lent) and celebration times (Christmas and Easter). Some children in the choir may be preparing for first reconciliation and first eucharist. These celebrations can provide valuable experiential learning opportunities that will help the whole choir understand the liturgical year and the sacraments of the church. Do not overlook these teachable moments. Help the choristers understand their role as liturgical ministers. Take time to build the foundation of the future church. Instill in them a love of ministerial service and an understanding of the Christian call to serve, and they will be active in music or other ministry throughout their lives.

Use the repertoire of each season to teach the regular rhythm of the liturgical year — Advent • Christmas • Epiphany; Lent • Easter Triduum • Eastertide; Ordinary Time. Build a repertoire that deepens an understanding, for example, of the text of a responsorial psalm or of the community's involvement in the communion procession. Dialogue with the children, explore possibilities and keep them interested. You will be surprised by what you both will learn.

Spiritual Development

A children's liturgical choir is not complete without a sense of prayer; this is the difference between a children's church choir and a secular school choir. They may have equal musicianship and even similar repertoire, but the difference is in the way they come together to pray and serve. Expose the group to many types of prayer, including formal prayer ("Hail, Mary," "Our Father," "Apostles' Creed") and more spontaneous intercessory prayer, such as the Prayer of the Faithful at liturgy. Explore how the different types of prayer are used in the celebration of liturgy on Sunday. Stir their creativity and encourage them to compose a liturgical prayer that they could use when they gather to rehearse or perform. Write it down, frame it for the choir room and have them pray it regularly. This will give them another opportunity for ownership and group identity.

In the process of rehearsing music, teaching music theory, exploring the liturgy and praying with the choir, the key word is *balance*. A world out of balance falls apart; so, too, a children's choir program. Balance work with fun, instruction with dialogue, discipline with laughter. Be open to the children and they will be open to you. Build mutual trust and confidence. Acknowledge the children's accomplishment with enthusiasm, giving them praise when it is due and corrective criticism when it is necessary. Reach for excellence; set a high standard. No one travels anywhere without a little expectation and a lot of prodding. A gentle sense of competition within the group is not a bad thing; it can help keep choristers on the "performance edge" during rehearsals as well as performances. Be ready to pick up those who may fall and quickly get them back to the group. The longer a lost sheep wanders, the farther it strays from the group.

As children develop the needed skills and make progress in musicianship, they need recognition and reinforcement. Building an achievement level program for choir members will allow public recognition of their accomplishments, reinforce their understanding of musicianship and ability with musical tools, and provide tangible evidence for parents of their child's success. Tangible awards for intangible advances provides child and parent with a healthy pride and sense of achievement.

The
Choral Sound

Chapter

The Choral Sound

"We sing a myst'ry from the past in halls that saints have trod,
Yet ever new the music rings to Jesus, Living Song of God."

"Eye Has Not Seen"
— Marty Haugen, b. 1950

As a director, your homework is never complete, your preparation never over. Along with conducting skills and teaching methodology, your education must include a sense of the choral sound you wish to produce. In order to have the children produce a good choral sound, you must first develop your own ear, filling your head with the sounds of many good children's choirs.

One way of doing this is to invest in recordings of excellent children's choirs from around the world. Each group will reflect its director's style as well as different styles of music. Listen carefully to the musicianship on these tapes and CDs; note what your choir can implement now or aspire to in the future. Listen critically, and write down the positive characteristics of each recorded group, noting also the drawbacks and limitations. What do you want your choir to imitate? What will you work to avoid? Educating your own ear and developing a clear sense of style gives substance to your vision for the choir.

At performances by children's choirs, both amateur and professional, you can observe the group's director in action. Take notes. How is the director's rapport with the children? How are the group's musical strengths reinforced by selection of repertoire? How are intonation problems and other musical difficulties handled by the choir and its director? Such performances are a classroom in which you can learn a great deal. If possible, talk to the conductor afterwards; ask questions about the performance and the possibility of attending a working rehearsal of the group.

Don't treat lightly an invitation to another conductor's rehearsal, or pass it up. What a golden opportunity for you to learn insights and techniques that you won't find in books and tapes! Remember your professional manners and be as unobtrusive as possible. Offer no comment unless requested by the director. You are the student in your colleague's classroom; use your time efficiently and effectively. Observe: How well does the group read music? What areas of musicianship — phrasing, intonation, harmonic difficulties — does the director concentrate on? Does the director use techniques that you might adapt? Save questions until after the rehearsal.

An excellent way to learn about the voice is to take voice lessons yourself. Do your research; ask colleagues to suggest a reputable teacher. (You'll find the same name or names keep coming up.) The purpose of your voice lessons is not to make you an opera star but to give you a better understanding of voice production. Becoming a student gives you insight into your choristers' vocal problems. It is difficult to be a director unless you can use your own voice confidently and with good musicianship.

The drawback is that lessons are expensive. If you cannot afford lessons, read books on voice production. You will find similarities and differences between children's and adult voices. Capitalize on the similarities and use them in your warm-up exercises and rehearsals.

Warm-up exercises These provide the foundation for making music and prevent problems from surfacing later. Avoid an academic approach to vocal exercises; children will be more interested and motivated by fun. Having them pant like a dog helps them find good breath support — which is crucial to solid tone production and good intonation. Working with lots of yawning helps children understand the concept of the open throat — which keeps the tone free and pleasant. Children often sing easily in the chest voice, or middle range; it's comfortable, requires a minimum of work and is usually near the pitch of their speaking voice. Hooting or fire engine exercises allow children to experiment freely and uninhibitedly with their upper range. The open, clear sound of a child's head voice is a memorable and uplifting sound. Help the children to make the transition from chest voice to head voice without stress or strain. Taking the time to develop the upper range will bring the children rewards of musicianship and confidence.

Pitch problems Some children come to choir with pitch problems. These difficulties can be cleared up with focused ear training. Don't limit yourself to using the piano for pitch work and music learning. When you are demonstrating a particular section, use your own voice — a cappella. (This is where your voice lessons will come in handy.) Some children may find it easier to match pitch with a voice, flute or baroque recorder rather than with a piano or synthesizer. Expose the choir to a variety of pitch timbres (sound types).

Sight reading There are several ways to begin the process of sight reading. The first step is to integrate brief sight reading skills into your regular warm-up at rehearsal. The various methods — solfège, numbers, Kodály — are simply tools. The director needs to feel comfortable and confident in whatever method is selected. Use a consistent teaching method, and use the sight singing exercises to reinforce the music being rehearsed. Fluctuating between methods causes confusion in the choir and breeds unrest.

Lost souls Every choir has a "lost" singer, one who is unsure of pitch or rhythm, or is just not quite "with the program."

Develop a buddy system, pairing a strong, experienced chorister with the weaker, unsure singer. The weaker ones' peers can keep them on the right track without constant supervision from the director (and without their feeling that they're being "picked on" by the director). For really difficult cases, private tutorials or small group singing lessons may help bring them up to the choir's standard. A talented parent may be able to work with these children if you can't squeeze in the time.

Air problems Many children have too much air and too little tone, or not enough air to keep the sound going for the full value of the phrase. There are a number of ways to solve air problems. Blowing up balloons is one way; it is extremely difficult not to use your diaphragm while doing this. Having the children play kazoos helps them with breath control: too much breath negates the kazoo's sound. A baroque recorder might be used to demonstrate tone production and allow the children to discover how delicately the breath must be controlled to make a well-supported tone. They will be able to see that the singing voice needs the same kind of breath support as the recorder does.

As noted in Chapter 4, children love using their breath to make a candle flame dance without blowing the candle out; it's tricky, but it's fun. "Humming with the bees" for an extended time uses the same skills. A "tone-holding contest" can help the children learn the importance of using their air efficiently and effectively to produce tones. Videotapes produced for children's choir directors can continue to give you examples and techniques for tone production. (See Appendix B, Resources.)

Rhythm Today's children usually have a keen sense of rhythm, thanks to popular music and reggae. Constant exposure keeps their rhythmic vocabulary diverse and complex. However, if difficulties arise, use brief echo clapping to reinforce understanding, slowly extending the process to longer phrases and more complex patterns. Another help is the use of rhythm word chants, which can often be found in the selected repertoire. Don't limit your creativity — or that of the choristers.

From Unison to Harmony

Unison Unison singing requires precision, so don't discount this part of the choristers' training. Have them open their ears and listen carefully and constructively. Good unison requires care and persistence; it is where confidence and excellence begin. A high standard for unison will make easier the movement into part singing, which requires confidence wedded to solid musicianship.

Rounds (canons) Once solid musical unison is established, the first step into harmony is singing familiar songs or hymns, or scale patterns, in a round or canon. Some examples are "Amazing Grace" (NEW BRITAIN), "The King Shall Come" (MORNING SONG), or TALLIS CANON (various texts). Interweaving these melodies is preparatory to singing in parts. Use rounds creatively during rehearsal, performances or liturgies. You might, for instance, start one of these hymns with congregation and choir; on the third or fourth verse, direct the children's choir to enter the round at the prescribed measure. Another way is to present as a reflection a familiar song or hymn sung in canon by the children's choir. Search out repertoire that will reinforce this step of the training process, in which choristers learn a sense of independence and become ready for part singing.

Partner songs and quodlibets These present another technique for beginning harmonic singing. Partner songs use two familiar songs that can be layered on top of one another in such a manner that pleasant harmonies are produced. It's also possible to find repertoire that uses this technique with freshly composed melodies, for example, "One Spirit, One Church" (Kevin Keil), "Here I Am" (Dan Schutte) and "Play before the Lord" (Bob Dufford). There is abundant repertoire available to support your musical and educational objectives. Be persistent; talk to colleagues.

Another technique is the use of "extended phrases" with echo harmonies, for example, the verses of "Hosea" (Carey Landry). This helps develop breath control for the extended supportive phrases and also helps tune the ear for harmony singing. In addition to the echo phrasing, you may want to teach the children a descant line to sing with a hymn or song sung by the adult choir. Like round singing, this can be great fun for all involved.

An easy step on the road to harmonic singing is thirds. Teach the third down and up during warm-up exercises at rehearsal. Repetition helps tune the choristers' ears to the third, one of the crucial tones in harmonic singing. A half-step makes the difference between major and minor — a pleasant tone or a tone cluster! Work for precision and well-supported tones. Tuning the ears and mind makes for alert singing, which produces intelligent musicians with a pleasant sound who are able to interpret the repertoire with sensitivity.

Sight singing Teaching sight singing is a responsibility of every music director, no matter whether the choir is made up of adults or children. Every rehearsal must employ some degree of sight singing; the more it is used, the better the skill is developed. Teaching by rote or spoon-feeding singers is the quick fix, but it stunts the developing skills of choristers and turns their minds off — and makes room for discipline problems!

When beginning sight singing, start with easy material. Read the music for tempo and dynamics. Walk the choir through a selection and ask their help with interpretation signs. Keep their heads, eyes, ears and voices engaged.

If you have used a series of warm-up exercises, write them out so that children can *see* the connection to the music they are preparing. Make the connection clear and the choir will follow. Look for hymn tunes and songs that have triadic opening phrases; connect them to triad exercises. Use the grand staff on the blackboard to help them see repeated tones and neighbor tones. Allow the children to construct melodies using these tones. Always connect the visual with vocal production.

Help choristers who play a musical instrument connect this vocal learning to their instrumental experience. Don't neglect the creative use of silence — the rest — however long or short. Have the children read with precision and care.

Developing strong, confident singers is not easy, and it doesn't happen overnight. Your courage, consistency and dedication will build intelligent musicians who will be able to communicate expressively with music. You must have a finely tuned ear yourself, as well as adequate music skills and abundant energy; most importantly, you need a clear idea of the choral sound you desire from your group. Don't leave it to chance, or it will sound chancy.

Repertoire

Repertoire | Chapter

"When in our music God is glorified. . ."

— Fred Pratt Green, b. 1903

Take great care in selecting music for children's choir. Your selections will have great impact on your choristers' development of taste and appreciation of different styles, which begins in childhood years. In reviewing songs, anthems or psalm settings, here are five points to consider:

Craftsmanship How is the music constructed? Is the tessitura (range) within the capabilities of the children's voices? A range of an octave, or an octave and a third, is reasonable; but an octave and a fifth might be too big a stretch for children. Would this piece expand the music vocabulary of the choir? Does the melody create interest and engage the ear?

Do the harmonies adequately support and complement the creative ideas of the melody? Are they varied enough to keep the children's ear alive and active? Will these harmonies confuse the children? Is there redundancy or triteness? Children will lose interest quickly if the music speaks down to them, if it does not engage and challenge them in the music making process. Boring music creates boring sounds and leads to poor musicianship and discipline problems. While selection of repertoire is often subjective, depending on the director's tastes and the community's needs, don't settle for anything less than solid musicianship and sturdy texts.

Text Is the text *worth* singing? Sunshine, flowers, rainbows and happiness are pleasant visual images for children, but are these images supported by age-appropriate theological substance? Read the texts carefully; question the theology they express, and make sure that it is what the Church teaches. Is the text grammatically correct? If not, chuck it out. Teaching beautiful tunes with solid theology and poor grammar is a bad choice for a children's choir. Do words and phrases have the natural flow of speech rhythms, or do they conflict with melody and rhythm? Avoid bad poetry and gender-specific language. Use texts with vocabulary that enriches rather than limits their understanding of theological concepts.

Flexibility Can this piece be recycled, i.e., used in many ways? How much "bang for the buck" can we get out of this music? How will it fit into the liturgical needs of the choir and community, and how will it fit into the concert schedule? Selecting music that wears well and can be re-used is a wise use of the music library budget, avoiding the silent reproach of dusty file folders filled with useless expense.

Consider also the musical style of the community. If everything is the same style, that's likely to become boring. Select a variety of styles: traditional and folk, unison and two-part, a cappella and with accompaniment. Shock has value, but something that's too far out may produce negative reactions. Make sure the risk is worth taking.

Imagination Does this piece energize the creativity of choristers and director? Can instrumentalists be added for a festive arrangement? Can the children contribute with additional harmonies, handbells, Orff instrumentation or rhythm instruments? A variety of performance options will lengthen an anthem's performance life in the choir and in the community.

Prayer How will this selection help choristers, assembly and director pray at liturgy or in performance? Is the style of prayer part of the vocabulary of the community, or will people "watch the performance" rather than participate in prayer?

Hymns

Directors of children's choirs often overlook one of the most valuable resources at their disposal: the hymn. A sense of history and tradition can disappear in a deluge of new tunes and catchy popular rhythms. This is not to say that traditional is "better" than contemporary or vice versa but, rather, that it is important to balance both styles within the context of children's choir repertoire. A well-sung hymn with a sturdy text, invigorating rhythms and attractive harmonies can provide as much excitement as an anthem in contemporary style using the same text.

"Hymns are boring!" Of course they are — if they're played with disregard for text. Presented with a vigorous tempo, a robust hymn can create interest and even excitement in the choristers. Hymns must be presented in a tempo that reflects their text: "O God, You Search Me" (Bernadette Farrell) would be sung more reflectively than "Joyful, Joyful, We Adore Thee" (HYMN TO JOY).

"Hymns have too many notes and too many words for children." Too many words? Just listen to the rap and pop tunes youngsters can sing! What *is* crucial is the way the director presents the hymn to the children. Any tune can be broken down into sections that children can learn at their own level with judicious repetition. Creative teaching and genuine enthusiasm are contagious. A director who communicates a lack of interest, openly or covertly, deprives children of part of their musical heritage.

In the process of learning a hymn, the child is exposed to poetic text, literary style and expanded vocabulary. The melody can often be used with other texts, easily expanding the repertoire with minimal investment of time and energy! (See Appendix D, Using a Metrical Index.)

Teaching a well-thought-out repertoire of hymns to the children's choir throughout the liturgical year provides a sense of history and vision. "O Come, O Come, Emmanuel" (VENI EMMANUEL) is written in a refrain style familiar in contemporary musical vocabulary, especially responsorial psalms; working through a few selected verses, children learn the history of the "O" Antiphons and become familiar with the numerous titles used for the Messiah in the Hebrew Scriptures. The director might consider presenting this hymn in conjunction with "My Soul in Stillness Waits" (Marty Haugen) to allow the children to experience settings of similar texts in diverse musical styles. Both combine well-constructed melody lines with chant style — in a sense, the pop tunes of the fifth century church.

In a similar manner, the first verse of "The First Noël" gives children some gospel infancy stories in a nutshell. The familiar refrain style makes it easy to learn. The *"Gloria"* refrain of "Angels We Have Heard on High" makes an excellent year-round warm-up exercise; repeat several times, each time a half-step higher.

As the children's choir continues through the liturgical year, hymns appropriate to each season are plentiful. The Lenten hymn "The Glory of These Forty Days" (ERHALT UNS HERR, LM) uses a fine poetic text to outline the perspectives of prayer and fasting in both the Hebrew and Christian Scriptures. The exuberant joy of the Easter season is found in "Jesus Christ Is Risen Today" (EASTER HYMN 77 77 with alleluias).

The hymn form has been used in the Roman tradition, especially at Morning Prayer (Lauds) and Evening Prayer (Vespers). In liturgical traditions today, opportunities to sing hymns are limited by the specific demands of the rites. This limitation may be a blessing in disguise, because too much hymn singing can be as draining as an excess of any musical style. A hymn may be used as an opening or closing song, or as a song of praise after communion, in which case there can be an instrumental recessional. Singing several verses of a hymn brings the assembly together and unifies it. At large celebrations such as Christmas or a service of Lessons and Carols, each stanza of a hymn may be sung differently: by assembly and choirs in unison, by the adult choir, by the children's choir, by everyone singing the final stanza together. What a wonderful expression of the unity of the family of faith!

Children's choir directors in Catholic churches are to follow the guidelines set forth in the *Constitution on the Sacred Liturgy* of the Second Vatican Council and the *Directory for Masses with Children* as well as three documents by the National Conference of Catholic Bishops of the United States of America: *Introduction to the Lectionary for Masses with Children, Music in Catholic Worship* and *Liturgical Music Today.* (These are available in *The Liturgy Documents,* Chicago: Liturgy Training Publications, 800.933.1800, or through OCP.)

Music is a language that goes beyond words to the heart and mind, communicating emotional expression and spiritual understanding. Music can engage singers' ministerial skills and empower assembly members in their "full, conscious and active participation in liturgical celebrations called for by the very nature of the liturgy." Such music is prayer.

Remember that choristers are ministers of music in the same way as adult singers or instrumentalists. Treat them as such when selecting repertoire, and they will feel a sense of vital contribution to the community's prayer life. You may find one song or hymn that works particularly well in producing a sense of prayer within the choir; this could become a signature piece for the group as a sung prayer to close rehearsal or as a warm-up piece before performances. Coming together in prayer is one of the hallmarks of a children's choir; it is an opportunity that many children will experience nowhere else.

Stretching the Budget

The money crunch leads to tough decisions. Music budgets are often limited, if they exist at all! This can be frustrating, but can also spur your creativity. Find one good anthem per term, and then rely on the parish hymnal or songbook. Go through the book, writing down a "dream list" of songs and hymns you'd like your community to learn; then review the list with the children's choir in mind. Could one of these songs serve as a unison anthem? Could another deepen the children's understanding of a liturgical season?

For example, "Sing Out, Earth and Skies" (Marty Haugen) allows the children's choir to split into antiphonal sections and join collectively on the refrain with the written descants. "On Our Journey to the Kingdom" (Tobias Colgan) is a stalwart hymn text with a varied vocabulary for children. The director can use it as an example of melodic contour as well as of the theology of the individual and community journey with Jesus, described in the process of Christian initiation. (See *Rite of Christian Initiation of Adults* [RCIA], especially sections 252–330, "Christian Initiation of Children Who Have Reached Catechetical Age.") For younger children (K–1) the repertoire might include a unison refrain from "Jesus, Come to Us" and "To Be Your Bread" (David Haas). Short refrains give younger children the opportunity for dialogue singing, with the director demonstrating good singing technique for the youngsters to imitate.

The repertoire should also include some special songs or anthems geared towards and prepared solely by the children's choir. These special songs must be challenging: it is better to stray on the road to the more difficult than to languish in the swamps of the too easy. Striking the correct balance is crucial in the first year. Be prepared for some winners and some losers among your choices. If you have chosen well, the winners will be in the repertoire next year and for years to come.

A number of seasonal anthems work well for children's choirs and have an innate motivational factor. "See amid the Winter's Snow" (Kevin Keil) gives children a wonderful study of major and minor tonality. "Christmastide Carol," by M.D. Ridge, is a solid teaching tool for Latin, and has two-part harmony that works well for grades three and up. "Thy Word," by Michael Smith, can provide more intricate rhythms and three-part harmonies to challenge more advanced singers.

Keep your eyes open for songs that are fun to sing yet teach musicianship and singing techniques. For more difficult rhythmic concepts, try the 5/4 meter of "Sing of the Lord's Goodness" (Ernest Sands). "Of the Father's Love Begotten" (DIVINUM MYSTERIUM) or "Lord of All Hopefulness" (SLANE) can strengthen melodic concepts; trying these a cappella can help fine tune a choir's listening skills.

Finding the repertoire that will fill your choir's needs and serve the prayer life for your community is like finding quality clothing: comfortable, attractive, well-fitting, appropriate and long-lasting. It takes time and an investment in thought and vision. Only you will know which of the huge range of selections on the market today will work with your group. Review carefully and thoughtfully, and you will build a solid library that will stand the test of time.

Parents and Volunteers

Chapter 10

Parents and Volunteers

"Ubi caritas et amor, Deus ibi est."

("Where charity and love are found,
God is there") — Latin chant

Parents are the *legs* of a children's choir program: It is next to impossible to build a successful program without getting parents involved — and keeping them involved. They provide a built-in public relations program; their word of mouth is a highly effective recruitment tool. Rely on them for constructive criticism and hands-on help.

The music and the children must be your primary focus. Save your energies; delegating to parents and volunteers the organizational and non-musical responsibilities avoids early burnout! One of the crucial questions a director must consider is, "Does this particular task need to be handled by me, or can it be better handled by someone else?"

Consider projects that might bring the parents together — just parents, without the children — to meet and talk with other parents of choristers. A Sunday welcome tea, a luncheon or a dessert-and-coffee evening provides a low-key social occasion when questions can be dealt with and car pool arrangements sorted out. Encourage parents to set up a phone tree to communicate vital information, such as unexpected schedule changes. The camaraderie begun in these social settings sets a positive tone for the months and years ahead. The bonds of community forged here continue to link many parents to the children's choir program long after their own children have graduated to adult music ministry. The director does not have to arrange such social occasions personally, but does need to attend; it's a great opportunity for a brief but brilliant talk about the program and a chance to affirm and encourage volunteers.

In the interview process (Chapter 4), you interviewed the parents as well as the children. Did you make notes on the parents' musical background and what their useful talents and gifts might be? Identify the parents' skills with care equal to that of selecting choristers or repertoire. Respect volunteer time as a highly valuable asset; it is not to be wasted. Give parents and volunteers projects that use their skills directly, efficiently and effectively. Put parents to work immediately as extra hands for rehearsal, in the library, at the music office and at receptions. A parental phone committee can follow up on absent choristers. Enthusiastic, conscientious parents can coordinate parties, potlucks, rehearsal snacks and receptions after concerts much more effectively than you; let them free you for the music making.

Technology Can Help

In this technological age, numerous parents are involved with computer work on a daily basis. Think of ways they can help with the children's choir program. If there is a parish database in place, that might be a starting point; a computer-savvy parent might be able to set up car pools, searching for children in the same neighborhood or region and helping parents coordinate their schedules.

Parents could keep track of a computer list of the choristers' birthdays; one might be in charge of purchasing birthday cards and postage and addressing the cards for a particular month. However, as director, you must take the time to write a personal note on the card. Children remember those who took a personal interest in their lives — who remembered a birthday or soccer game, or recognized a science award. Parents can help keep you current on children's extra-musical accomplishments.

Using the computer to organize the music library can be very helpful in classifying anthems and other music. For each title, you (or your computer volunteers) can make notes of liturgical use, performance frequency and level of difficulty.

Don't limit publicity to the conventional means of posters, pulpit announcements and the church bulletin. If the parish has a web page or home page on the Internet, use it; make it interesting and engaging for children as well as informational for parents. As a director, you might use the Internet to exchange thoughts about repertoire, performance techniques and recruitment ideas with other directors across the state, or the nation, or the world.

Fundraising

Funding for the children's choir needs to be addressed initially by the pastor, finance council and music director; it is best to have the financial parameters laid out in the preliminary steps of the program. Where will the money come from for music? For field trips? For choir materials? Once the needs and costs have been outlined, look to parents to do the fundraising (if this is necessary, and if the parish permits it). Projects for financial support of the program — organizing a golf tournament, selling magazine subscriptions — should not be micromanaged by the children's choir director. Parents may already have both the contacts and the organizing skills to make fundraising efforts effective.

Whether your children's choir is just starting out or is well established, use the parents' talent to make the program family-involved. This is the best foundation for future successes.

Expanding the Horizons

Expanding the Horizons | Chapter

11

*"On our journey to the kingdom
Forward goes our pilgrim band."*

— Bernhardt Severin Ingemann, 1789–1862
tr. Sabine Baring-Gould, 1834–1924

The children's choir program is part of the parish music ministry. Once the program is on a solid footing, you may want to present the choristers with additional challenges.

A joint concert or liturgy with the adult music ministry of the parish can energize both programs. The adults see future musicians at work with them, and children get a sense of what a larger sound feels like. A joint repertoire and performance presents music ministry as a community event rather than fragmented groups. The director will have a larger group to conduct and a different sound to shape. Creating the desired sound will be a challenge that stretches both director and choristers, but it's well worth the effort.

As the program develops, extended works on biblical themes, classical cantatas, and sacred works are possibilities that might be undertaken with the adult choir or with choirs from neighboring parishes. A cantata based on bible stories is a great source of musical challenge, theological training, ensemble theatre — and fun! What child (for that matter, what adult) doesn't like costumes and a little greasepaint? But drama, set design and costumes are extras. Do not lose track of quality musicianship as the heart of the program; without a strong heartbeat, a program will quickly die. A large performing group can work on more difficult music while broadening the child's vision of church community.

Taking It on the Road

"Taking the show on the road" solidifies the choir, gives members pride in their work and builds awareness of the parish and ministry to the community. A trip to the diocesan cathedral can be a source of excitement and enthusiasm. Talk to the music director in advance: can your group sing at one of the cathedral liturgies? Assist with service music? Present a formal concert?

Singing a liturgy, concert or joint performance at the cathedral with the parish adult choir can provide many a teachable moment for the choristers. The history of the Catholic church in the region, the role of the bishop, the history and architecture of the diocesan church and its role in liturgical life. Many diocesan cathedrals are acoustically vibrant places to sing; this can be a real "ear-opener" for choristers who usually sing in a suburban church with relatively flat acoustics. Don't limit the concert to music that covers the cathedral's architectural period; think of covering the historical periods of the church's development within the region. Such diocesan visits give children a sense of belonging to the larger church as well as the parish.

A local or regional concert tour can test the waters to see if the group has the stamina necessary for longer trips. Consider a joint tour with a neighboring parish to provide cross-pollination and fellowship among the different choirs. Rural parishes might be happy to host a visit from the children's choir; both host parish and visiting choir can experience the joys of Christian hospitality and good will. Performances in different local or regional churches give choristers a chance to perform in different acoustics, participate in different liturgical styles and possibly speak and sing in different languages. The language of music bridges differences. These experiences can help choristers become well-rounded people with a balanced perspective on life.

Look also at the possibility of hosting a visiting choir in your home parish. Choristers who take an active part will learn valuable lessons; they will be able to observe a different director and choir in rehearsal; they will hear the different types of sound that another choir produces. You will learn, too, from seeing how another director works and from talking together about repertoire, interpretation, intonation problems and special techniques for successful approaches to difficult musical concepts.

Be selective about invitations for your choir to sing in other venues; not all venues or invitations are of equal benefit to the children or others. Remember the dignity and purpose of the choir you are directing. Do not allow the social pressures of the season, parish or community to exploit the children's mission. Your choice can deepen the children's sense of ministry: a cathedral is a much better musical experience than Christmas caroling in a shopping mall. Sing at a nursing home in the spring rather than cramming the visit in during the Christmas rush. If possible, a personal on-site visit well in advance of the concert or liturgy will help avoid pitfalls, conflicts and unwelcome surprises for you and your choristers. Avoid shopping malls, busy hotel lobbies and other areas where your choir's performance will be treated as mere background music. Stick to your standards.

Prayer Life of the Children's Choir

Chapter 12

Prayer Life of the Children's Choir

"Let the children come to me;
do not hinder them,
for God's reign belongs to such as these."

— Mark 10:14

The children's choir program is vitally connected to the prayer life of the worshiping community it is called to serve. This is the primary difference between the children's choir of a church and that of a secular community. You, as director, must develop the foundation of prayer in addition to knowing the skills and preparing the music.

Computers and video games have sharpened children's reaction time, but do nothing to develop the expression of feelings among a group. Help the children through this window of expression with music, giving them a tool to express emotions constructively and creatively. Rehearsal schedules may not permit extended periods of prayer; use the time you have to evoke a prayer response from the children, as individuals and as a group.

A parent may have a particular gift of prayer or be able to assist with prayer experiences. Talk about it in advance, to ensure that you and the parent have complementary views on prayer, faith and their articulation.

Encourage the children to write "a chorister's prayer" that might be used as an opening or closing prayer for each rehearsal. Help them to explore a variety of prayer styles: formal prayer (e.g., "Our Father," "Hail, Mary"), spontaneous intercessory prayer (asking God in their own words) or mantra prayer that might use a Taizé-style sung refrain. Your investment in the children's prayer life will have a powerful effect on your own. A child's simple prayer can bring wonderful focus to a stressed-out director. Every rehearsal should end with some form of prayer. Every liturgy or concert should begin with prayer; it is as necessary as a vocal warm-up.

During the year, a number of your choristers may be involved in sacramental preparation programs: first communion, first reconciliation, and Christian Initiation of Children Who Have Reached Catechetical Age (see RCIA), or the Anointing of the Sick. Their fellow choristers can become involved as individuals and as a group by praying for them at rehearsal and participating in the liturgies. When choir members choose prayer partners, the experience can bring significance to their prayer life, particularly for children preparing for sacramental celebration.

There may come a time when a child's family is experiencing a death, a military deployment, a life-threatening illness or other grave difficulty. The experience of music and prayer during rehearsal can be a great comfort to that child, as is the knowledge that others are praying for the family. In today's violent society, music and prayer can help children express feelings they may be called on to identify much too early in life: the death of other children by shooting, the death of a teacher or fellow student. Music could diffuse or even prevent some violence and destruction. Sometimes the pastor or an associate might attend rehearsal and pray with the choir. Having a guest at rehearsal is a great motivator and, in the eyes of a child, the presence of the pastor is like a visit from the President.

In the process of helping prepare the children's prayer life, do not forget your own. Taking time in the quiet of your heart will make for focused rehearsals and well-prepared performances. Prayer is not a substitute for good rehearsals and musical preparation, but it is an integral part of them. Allow your prayer to become your song, and your song to become prayer. It is a powerful expression that affects both those who sing and those who listen.

Summary: End-of-the-Year Inventory

After the first choir season — September to May, or another schedule suitable for your community — give yourself a pat on the back. Congratulations! Take a deep breath and relax. Now you need to take inventory of what you and your choir have accomplished in this first season.

What music skills have the children developed, refined or re-defined? What did you learn from them? (Learning is a two-way street.) Can they now match pitch, sing a third and a fifth in tune? Can they read and sing a four-stanza hymn? Do they understand the musical road maps? Do they know where to go at the end of a verse or refrain, or when it says *"D.C. al fine"*?

Do they sing the text with expression and appropriate dynamics? Are their minds engaged in music making? During rehearsal has their attention span lengthened and concentration improved? How have they fared in their first steps of sight singing? Do they pray well together in word and song?

If the answer is yes, give thanks and praise to God! You have taught the children, touching their hearts and minds. All of you have grown in the process, which will affect your lives for years to come, as well as future involvement in liturgical music ministry.

If the children have learned to interact positively with one another, then you have helped them on their journey of working within the community. If choir members have come to a sense of prayer, given examples of gospel values or sung psalms and hymns of praise from the heart, count yourself blessed for being an instrument. What a privilege to help them communicate with God and experience the love of Jesus and the prompting of the Holy Spirit!

How have the choristers affected the prayer life of the community they have been called to serve? Have they been integrated into the liturgical life of the church, giving support and not calling undue attention to themselves or their performance?

As director, how have you fared in keeping your life in balance with the demands of the children's choir program? Have your teaching methods grown to meet the needs of the choir? What new ways have you found to communicate with the children and their parents? Have you continued to practice diplomacy and tact amid rehearsals, liturgy, special projects and concerts?

Behind every child is at least one parent. Have you discovered more helpful ways to engage the talents of parents in support of the program or to expand it? Have parents taken a more active role in music ministry because of their contact with the children's choir program and your personal invitation?

Have church staff members gained a better insight into the importance of the children's choir program through the children's active role at worship and work within the community? Have staff members shared ideas and visions that might help the program? Everyone loves to give advice; listen gratefully and discern what may enhance next year's program. For instance, working together with the religious education program might help increase the children's involvement in the choir program — and vice versa!

These are just a few questions for you to reflect on as the first year comes to a close. Now, write down the three most successful events of this past year: ones that gave you energy or reinforced your vision with the excitement to move ahead. Capitalize on these successes; they will nourish your dreams and visions for the future of the program.

Then look at three events that failed. Be honest in analyzing why they did not work and who or what may have caused the failure. Be not the first to criticize nor the last to accept responsibility, but be open and honest with yourself. A staff member you trust may be able to help with this process.

Look to the future, setting goals for next year in the light of what has happened this year. You may need to adjust your compass for the next few weeks, or refocus some three-year goals. A change in course can help alleviate stress; it can provide a more successful educational experience and a deeper ministerial response than grimly struggling to meet the original goals. Stay rooted in the moment; keep your mind open, alert to opportunities that can help the children's choir ministry. It may be time to take a conducting course or attend a summer music course at a nearby university. You might gather together three or four children's choir directors to brainstorm some ideas, writing them on index cards and keeping them handy for planning future choir activities.

A ship goes nowhere without a captain to set its course. Through thoughtful evaluation of the past year, set your course for the year ahead. Success is yours if you keep your goals clear as you journey with Jesus at your side.

The
Appendix

Appendix

Basic Terms

a cappella	(Italian: "in church style") singing without accompaniment
anthem	short choral piece not intended to be sung by the assembly; a selection sung by the choir
canon	composition in which a melody is repeated by overlapping other voice parts; the most familiar type of canon is the *round*
chest voice	lower portion of a singer's range; tones that resonate in the chest
choir	group of singers, especially one that performs in church
chorister	member of a choir
chromatic	proceeding by half tones; including notes not belonging to a given major or minor key
diaphragm	internal muscle, separating the chest from the abdomen, used in breathing
dynamics	The softness or loudness with which music is performed; ranges from *pianissimo* (very soft; *pp, ppp*) to *fortissimo* (very loud; *ff, fff*). Other common dynamic score markings include: *crescendo (cres., cresc.)* gradually louder *decrescendo (decr., decresc.)* gradually softer *diminuendo (dim.)* gradually softer *forte (f)* loud *mezzo forte (mf)* moderately loud *mezzo piano (mp)* moderately soft *piano (p)* soft
grand staff	treble staff and bass staff together, usually joined by a brace

harmony	sounds in combination (see *unison*)
head voice	upper portion of a singer's range; tones that resonate in the head
hymn	song or poem praising God; a metrical song for assembly singing
hymn tune	melody of a hymn; the name of a particular hymn melody; more than one text may be sung to a particular hymn tune; see Appendix D, Using a Metrical Index.
intonation	performer's accuracy with respect to pitch
Kodály, Zoltan	Hungarian composer (1992–1967) who believed that all children should take part in choral singing; also the music teaching method named for him
melody	group of successive musical tones that make up a meaningful whole; a melody that can be sung is often called a tune
meter	arrangement of beats in measures with regularly recurring accents
metrical index	listing of hymn tunes by meter (e.g., in a hymnal)
neighbor tone	a pitch one step higher or lower than the one it precedes and the one it follows
octave	distance between a given pitch and the note eight scale degrees above or below it
octavo	published booklet containing the sheet music for a choral composition
Orff instruments	percussion instruments developed by German composer Carl Orff (1895–1982) for use in his system of musical instruction for children

part-singing	singing of music with more than one voice part
partner song	two different songs that can be sung simultaneously, creating harmony (see *quodlibet*)
pitch	the highness or lowness of a musical tone
quodlibet	composition in which two or more familiar melodies are put together so that they sound at the same time (see *partner song*)
repertoire	the stock of music that a choir is able to perform
rhythm	regular pattern formed by notes of differing stress and duration; also, notes in time, including meter (pattern of note duration), beat (pattern of accented notes) and tempo (rate of speed)
round	vocal composition of three or more parts that enter in sequence, each singing the same melody and words; the round is a form of *canon*
sight reading, sight singing	skill of playing or singing a piece of music at first sight without preparation
solfeg, solfège, solfeggio	musical training involving ear training and sight singing, using sol-fa syllables to represent the notes of the scale: do-re-mi-fa-sol-la-ti-do
synthesizer	electronic instrument, played with a keyboard, that produces sounds including sounds similar to other instruments
tessitura	the prevailing range of a vocal or instrumental part

third	the third degree of a scale; the middle note of a triad; the interval between the first and third tones in a scale
timbre	the distinctive quality of a sound or tone; pron. *tam'br*
tone	a sound of distinct pitch, quality and duration
treble voicing	choral music arranged for the highest voice parts
triad	chord or cluster of three notes, made up of two thirds: The bottom note is the root, middle note is the third, and top note is the fifth.
unison	all voices singing the same voice part together
voicing	choral music arranged for different combinations of voices, e.g., SATB (soprano, alto, tenor, bass), SSA (first soprano, second soprano, alto), SAB (soprano, alto, baritone), etc.

Appendix

B

Resources

Bartle, Jean Ashworth. *Lifeline for Children's Choir Directors,* Revised Edition. Toronto, Ontario: Gordon V. Thompson Music, 1993.

Strong outline of vocal training for children's voices, geared towards school children's choir and community children's choir. Large section on repertoire, both sacred and secular.

Bertalot, John. *Five Wheels to Successful Sight Singing: A Practical Approach to Teach Children (and Adults) to Read Music.* Minneapolis MN: Augsburg Fortress, 1993.

As the title states, a practical approach to teaching sight singing and developing musicians' skills. A companion video prepared for use with this book effectively reinforces the technique with visual demonstrations.

John Bertalot. *Immediately Practical Tips for Choral Directors.* Minneapolis MN: Augsburg Fortress. 1994.

Geared toward the director of a complete choir program. The diary format makes for easy, engaging reading, with accessible tips for directors of any education or experience.

Both Bertalot's books are required reading for master's programs in a number of American universities and music schools.

Church Music for Children series. Nashville TN: Abingdon Press, 1996

Church Music for Children: Pre-elementary (4–6 years), Eileen Jones Straw and Steve Pattison

Church Music for Children: Younger Elementary (Grades 1–3), David Bone and Ginger Wyrick

Church Music for Children: Older Elementary (Grades 4–6), John Horman and Angela Tipps

Church Music for Children: Combined Elementary (Grades 1–6), Timothy Edmonds

Series of manuals with lesson plans and projects outlined in a step-by-step process for the volunteer director. Methodist perspectives throughout. Cassette tapes are available for use with this program.

Haasemann, Frauke and Jordan, James M. *Group Vocal Technique.* Chapel Hill NC: Hinshaw Music, 1991.

Basic manual with strong technique for proper singing with adults which can be selectively transferred for use with children's voices. Deals with tone, posture and vocal exercise techniques. The manual is accompanied by a videotape that visually reinforces the techniques; manual and video need to be used in conjunction with one another.

Hill, David; Parfitt, Hilary, and Ash, Elizabeth. *Giving Voice: A Handbook for Choir Directors and Trainers.* Suffolk, U.K.: Kevin Mayhew, Ltd., 1995.

General introductory book that gives good outlines, provides warm-up exercises and ideas to assist with vocal projection, resonance and intonation. No training scheme or repertoire. A British publication with scholarly contributors at a layperson's reading level.

Jordan, James. *Evoking Sound: Fundamentals of Choral Conducting and Rehearsing.* Chicago: G.I.A. Publications, 1996.

Takes choral singing back to the basics of breath control and posture. Provides conducting skills and music inter-pretation. Focused on adult choirs, but has insights for children's choir directors. This resources is strong as a conductor's manual but limited on vocal technique.

Kemp, Helen. *Of Primary Importance,* Volumes 1 and 2. Garland TX: Choristers Guild, 1989. Distributors: Lorenz Corporation, Dayton OH.

Kemp, Helen. *Sing and Rejoice.* (videocassette) St. Louis MO: Concordia Publishing House, 1985.

Video by one of the masters. A bit dated, but the techniques for preparing and rehearsing the child's voice, as well as the philosophy of children's choirs, stand strong against present standards. Presents the Kemp perspective of the whole person — "body, mind and spirit" — as involved in music making.

McRae, Shirley W. *Directing the Children's Choir: A Comprehensive Resource.* New York: Schirmer Books, A Division of MacMillan, 1991.

A well-outlined book, helpful for the beginning children's choir director.

Page, Sue Ellen. *Hearts and Hands and Voices: Growing in Faith through Choral Music.* Tarzana CA: H.T. FitzSimons–Fred Bock Music, 1995.

Book strongly rooted in tradition and philosophy of the Choristers Guild, with well-thought-out process for setting up children's choir programs in the church community. Large section on development of choral tone in children. Brief section on conducting. Strong bibliography with references to specific interests.

Rotermund, Donald, ed. *Children Sing His Praise: A Handbook for Children's Choir Directors.* St. Louis MO: Concordia Publishing House, 1985.

Well-known children's choir contributors include Helen Kemp, Paul Bouman and Ronald Nelson. Focus on children's choir program in a Lutheran church setting. Brief historical summary of the children's choir, as well as suggestions for directing and for developing the vocal technique of children.

Stepping Stones: An Ecumenical Children's Choir Curriculum,
series editor, Michael C. Hawn. Garland TX: Choristers
Guild, 1995. Distributors: Lorenz Corp., Dayton OH.

Stepping Stones — Year 1: Early Childhood,
Ronald A. Nelson

Stepping Stones — Year 2: Early Childhood,
Randall McChesney

Stepping Stones — Year 3: Early Elementary,
Betty Bedsole

Stepping Stones — Year 4: Early Elementary,
Rebecca Gruber

Stepping Stones — Older Elementary,
Craig Singleton

Graded program that covers basic musicianship based
on Kodály methodology, in a three-year sequence with
cassette tapes, melodic cards and sign charts. Employs
hymnology and standard children's choir repertoire for
teaching material.

Stultz, Marie. *Innocent Sounds: Building Choral Tone and
Artistry in Your Children's Choir.* St. Louis MO: Morning
Star Music Publishers, 1999.

Choir director's manual for building good intonation
and formulating children's choir philosophy. Extensive
section on selection of repertoire and using the repertoire
to build good choral tone. A CD recording accompanies
the manual with examples.

Voice for Life. A complete, graduated training program for
children's choirs. Cleveland Lodge, Dorking, England
RH5 6BW: Royal School of Church Music, 1999. Email
voiceforlife@rscm.com Web site www.rscm.com.

Appendix C

Helpful Professional Organizations

Choristers Guild
2834 West Kingsley Road
Garland TX 75041

Royal School of Church Music in America
1361 West Market Street
Akron OH 44313

National Pastoral Musicians Association
225 Sheridan Street N.W.
Washington DC 20001-1492

American Choral Directors' Association
P.O. Box 6310
Lawton OK 73506-0310

American Guild of Organists, National Headquarters
475 Riverside Drive, Suite 1260
New York NY 10115

American Orff-Schulwerk Association
P.O. Box 18495
Cleveland Heights OH 44118

Music Educators' National Conference
106 Robert Fulton Drive
Reston VA 22091

Organization of American Kodály Educators
Music Dept. Box 2017
Nichols State University
Thibodaux LA 70310

**The American Boychoir Presser Treble Choral Music
Study Center**
19 Lambert Drive
Princeton NJ 08540

Dalcroze Society of America
Dr. Julia Schnebly-Black
University of Washington
2871 45th Street N.E.
Seattle WA 98105

Appendix

D

Using a Metrical Index

M.D. Ridge

Did you know that the words of "Amazing Grace" can be sung to the tune of the theme song from "Gilligan's Island"? It's true! Now, that's not something you'd want to use in the context of liturgy, but it illustrates two points: the words of one hymn can fit the tune of a completely different hymn; and a metrical index is one of the choir director's most useful tools.

First, some basic terms:
A **hymn tune** is the melody of a hymn. It will usually have a regular rhythm, or **meter**; it's sung from start to finish and then repeated for succeeding verses or **stanzas**. The tune can be long or short, but every stanza is the same length.

Hymn tunes have names; some are traditional names and others are named by the **composer** who wrote the tune. Most hymnals print the name of the tune either above or below the hymn. ("For All the Saints" is usually sung to Ralph Vaughan Williams' hymn tune SINE NOMINE. Williams must have had a good sense of humor, because the Latin SINE NOMINE means "without a name" in English.)

The **text** is the lyrics, or words, of a hymn. The writer of the text is called the **author.** The meter comes from the number of syllables in each line of the text. The number of lines in a stanza may vary from hymn to hymn; but in a given hymn, every stanza or verse has the same number of lines and the same number of syllables in each line.

"Joyful, Joyful, We Adore Thee," for instance, will usually have the following reference:
Text: 87 87 D; Henry van Dyke, 1852–1933
Tune: HYMN TO JOY; Ludwig van Beethoven, 1770–1827; adapt. by Edward Hodges, 1796–1867

The text reference gives the meter (87 87 D) with the author's name and dates. ("Alt." would indicate that the text has been altered — for instance, from "thee" and "thy" to "you" and "your.") The meter — 87 87 — indicates that the first and third lines have eight syllables; the second and fourth lines have seven syllables. The "D" means that the pattern is doubled, so that there are eight lines in each verse.

The music reference gives the hymn tune name; the composer's name and dates, and any other information about the tune.

Knowing the meter and the hymn tune name, you can turn to the **metrical index** often found in the back of the hymnal or in the accompaniment book; it should be listed in the table of contents.

The various meters are usually listed in numerical order. Look at the listing for 87 87 D. The "Metrical Index of Tunes" for *Glory and Praise,* Second Edition, for example, lists eight hymn tunes at 87 87 D:

ABBOT'S LEIGH

HYMN TO JOY

BEACH SPRING

HOLY ANTHEM

HYFRYDOL

IN BABILONE

NETTLETON

PLEADING SAVIOR

Say, for instance, that you like the text of "Alleluia! Alleluia! Let the Holy Anthem Rise" and want to use it for Easter — but your community doesn't know the HOLY ANTHEM tune, and there isn't time to teach it to them. Because HOLY ANTHEM and HYMN TO JOY have the same meter, you can sing the words of "Alleluia! Alleluia! Let the Holy Anthem Rise" to the tune of "Joyful, Joyful, We Adore You." Another example is "Lord, You Give the Great Commission"; it is a very useful hymn text that can readily be sung with the HYMN TO JOY tune if your community doesn't know the ABBOT'S LEIGH tune.

When substituting a tune, however, it's a good idea to sing the whole song through aloud (yes, every verse) to make sure the text and new tune fit together properly. Sometimes a dotted rhythm, or the change from one time signature to another, may result in accents on the wrong "sylLAble." Don't force a fit; if one tune doesn't work, try a different one in the same meter.

Some hymn tunes are unique in their meter; these may be listed as Irregular, or One of a Kind.

Some meters are abbreviated:

SM	SHORT METER	66 86
SMD	SHORT METER DOUBLE	66 86 66 86
CM	COMMON METER	86 86
LM	LONG METER	88 88

Sometimes a hymnal or worship aid will give only the hymn tune name. To find the meter, just count the number of syllables in each line. For example, if the first and third lines have eight syllables per line, and the second and fourth lines have six syllables per line, the tune is in 86 86, or Common Meter (CM). With that information, you can look up the tune name in any hymnal's metrical index.

You can see now why choir directors tend to collect lots of different hymnals; a good text on an unfamiliar tune may be singable with a more familiar tune, expanding the repertoire almost effortlessly. The names of tunes (HYFRYDOL, HYMN TO JOY, KINGSFOLD) eventually become as familiar as the title of the texts sung to them.

Standard Hymns

with hymn tune name and meter

ADVENT

O Come, O Come, Emmanuel VENI EMMANUEL, LM with
   refrain

The King Shall Come When Morning Dawns MORNING
   SONG, CM*

CHRISTMAS

Angels We Have Heard on High GLORIA 7777 with refrain
O Come, All Ye Faithful ADESTE FIDELES, Irregular with
   refrain

EPIPHANY

Songs of Thankfulness and Praise SALZBURG 77 77 D

LENT

Lord, Who throughout These Forty Days ST. FLAVIAN, CM
The Glory of These Forty Days ERHALT UNS HERR, LM

HOLY WEEK

O Sacred Head Surrounded PASSION CHORALE 76 76 D

EASTER

Jesus Christ Is Risen Today EASTER HYMN, 77 77 with alleluias
Now the Green Blade Rises NOEL NOUVELET, 11 10 10 11
Ye Sons and Daughters of the Lord O FILII ET FILIAE, 888
   with alleluias

PENTECOST

Come Down, O Love Divine DOWN AMPNEY, 66 11 D
Come, Holy Ghost LAMBILLOTTE, LM with repeat

GOD'S REIGN

All Creatures of Our God and King LASST UNS ERFREUEN, LM
    with alleluias
I Sing the Mighty Power of God ELLACOMBE, CMD, *or*
    MOZART, CMD
Joyful, Joyful, We Adore Thee HYMN TO JOY, 87 87 D

MARIAN

Ave Maria AVE MARIA, Irregular (chant)
Magnificat (Bernadette Farrell)

SAINTS

For All the Saints SINE NOMINE, 10 10 10 with alleluias*

* may be sung in canon